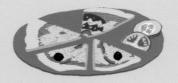

Rosa's Big Pizza Experiment

Child's Play (International) Ltd
Ashworth Rd, Bridgemead, Swindon SN5 7YD, UK
Swindon   Auburn ME   Sydney
ISBN 978-1-78628-554-6   L180121RW03215546

Printed in Heshan, China
3 5 7 9 10 8 6 4 2
www.childs-play.com

"Let's make pizza! Here's the recipe," says Rosa. "The ingredients for the dough are flour, yeast, salt and warm water."

"I've got the rolling pin. What else will we need?" asks Jamil.
"I like these measuring cups," says Sadiq.

"How much flour?" asks Kezia.
"Weigh some on the scales," Rosa answers.
"Here comes a flour cloud!" laughs Kezia.

Sadiq uses the cups to measure more flour. "1, 2, 3, 4, 5," counts Sadiq. Jamil checks the water level.

"I'll sprinkle in the dried yeast," says Rosa. "Yeast uses the flour to create bubbles," explains Jamil. "That's what makes the dough rise."

Kezia adds the warm water.
"Mixing it is fun!" laughs Sadiq.
"Mmm!" sniffs Jamil. "It smells delicious."

"Wow! Our ball of dough
is really heavy!" exclaims Rosa.
"Be careful it doesn't slip away,"
laughs Sadiq.

"How many pieces do we cut the dough into?" asks Rosa. "Four?" "Yes," agrees Kezia. "One piece each."

Squish! Squish!

Rosa and Jamil stretch
and knead their pizza dough.
"Boo!" laughs Rosa.

"Let's put the dough here to rest," says Kezia. "It will rise faster if it's warm."

"Oh dear, Jamil," says Sadiq. "Your dough hasn't risen very much."
"You can share ours," offers Rosa.

Thump!

"Choose your toppings," says Rosa. "Look!" growls Sadiq. "I've made a monster face!"

"If we set the timer, it will ring when the pizzas are cooked," says Rosa. "We don't want them to burn!"

"My pizza's really crunchy," says Jamil.
"You rolled your dough thinly," replies Kezia,
"so it cooked more quickly."

"Look how different our pizzas are," laughs Rosa. "But they all taste delicious."